A Note to Parent

D1461170

DK READERS is a compelling re~ children, designed in conjunction ~ ~~~~~y literacy experts, including Cliff Moon M.Ed., Honorary Fellow of the University of Reading. Cliff Moon has spent many years as a teacher and teacher educator specializing in reading and has written more than 140 books for children and teachers. He reviews regularly for teachers' journals.

Beautiful illustrations and superb full-colour photographs combine with engaging, easy-to-read stories to offer a fresh approach to each subject in the series. Each DK READER is guaranteed to capture a child's interest while developing his or her reading skills, general knowledge, and love of reading.

The five levels of DK READERS are aimed at different reading abilities, enabling you to choose the books that are exactly right for your child:

Pre-level 1 – Learning to read
Level 1   – Beginning to read
Level 2   – Beginning to read alone
Level 3   – Reading alone
Level 4   – Proficient readers

The "normal" age at which a child begins to read can be anywhere from three to eight years old, so these levels are only a general guideline.

No matter which level you select, you can be sure that you are helping your child learn to read, then read to learn!

LONDON, NEW YORK, DELHI,
MUNICH, and MELBOURNE

Series Editor Deborah Lock
Senior Art Editor Tory Gordon-Harris
Design Assistant Sadie Thomas
Production Claire Pearson
DTP Designer Almudena Díaz

Reading Consultant
Cliff Moon, M.Ed.

Published in Great Britian by
Dorling Kindersley Limited
80, The Strand, London WC2R ORL
2 4 6 8 10 9 7 5 3 1

A Penguin Company

A CIP record for this book is available
from the British Library

ISBN 0-7513-4398-6

Colour reproduction by Colourscan, Singapore
Printed and bound in China by L Rex Printing Co., Ltd.

The publisher would like to thank the following
for their kind permission to reproduce their photographs:
a=above; c=centre; b=below; l=left; r=right t=top;

Ardea London Ltd: 18-19; **Corbis:** Stephen Frink 16-17; Jeffrey L.
Rotman 26-27; **Getty Images**: AEF - Tony Malquist 12t, 28c; Pete
Atkinson 2-3; David Fleetham 20tl; Jeff Hunter 6-7, 30-31; Herwarth
Voigtmann 4-5t; **Nature Picture Library Ltd:** Constantino Petrinos 23tr;
N.H.P.A.: Pete Atkinson 14-15; **Oxford Scientific Films:** Tobias
Bernhard 10-11; **Science Photo Library:** GUSTO 4l.Jacket: **Getty
Images:** Stuart Westmorland front.

All other images © Dorling Kindersley
For further imformation see: www.dkimages.com

see our complete catalogue at
www.dk.com

DK READERS

LEARNING pre-level 1 TO READ

Fishy Tales

A Dorling Kindersley Book

Take a
swim in the
blue sea.

snorkel

clam

Here is a
coral reef.

coral

What can you see?

coral

fish

eye

fin

fish

spot

Small fish
are swimming
in and out
of the coral.

flipper

 turtles

The turtles
are playing
in the sea.

shell

tail

sea horses

fin

snout

The sea horses
are swaying
to and fro.

arm

 starfish

Starfish
are crawling
on the seabed.

tentacles

jellyfish

Jellyfish
are floating
up and down
in the sea.

bell

fin

tail

Here comes a shark
looking for food.

 sharks

mouth

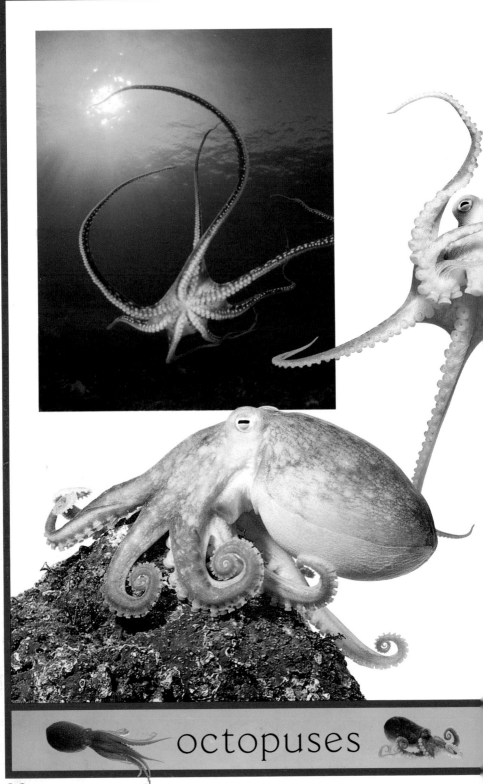

octopuses

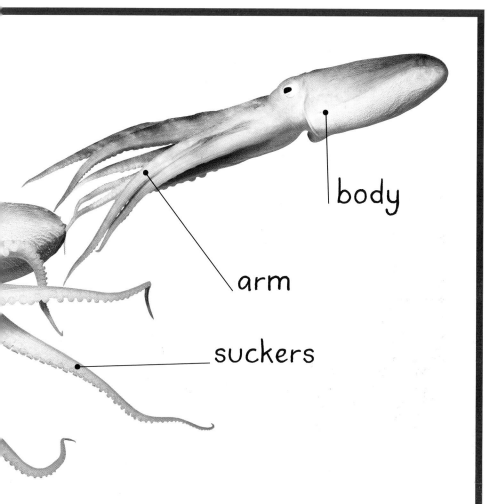

body

arm

suckers

An octopus is
zooming off
to hide.

claw

crabs

leg

Crabs are hiding in the coral and in big shells.

shell

23

tail

A ray is hiding
on the seabed.

rays

eye

fin

25

A dolphin is swimming away from the shark.

mouth

dolphins

tail

flipper

Eels are looking out for the shark.

tail

eels

fin

eye

The shark is
swimming away.

Can you see ...

fin

gills

nose

a fish ? coral ?

Picture word list

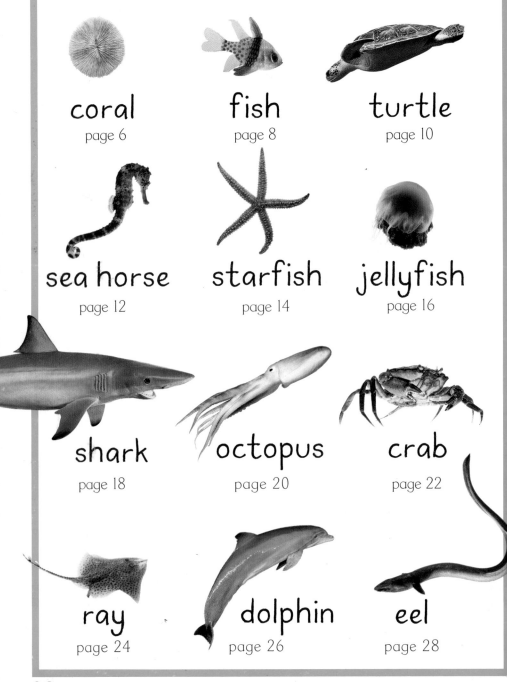

coral
page 6

fish
page 8

turtle
page 10

sea horse
page 12

starfish
page 14

jellyfish
page 16

shark
page 18

octopus
page 20

crab
page 22

ray
page 24

dolphin
page 26

eel
page 28